My First Sleepover

Charlotte Guillain

www.raintreepublishers.co.uk
Visit our website to find out more information about Raintree books.

To order:
☎ Phone 0845 6044371
🖹 Fax +44 (0) 1865 312263
🖳 Email myorders@raintreepublishers.co.uk

Customers from outside the UK please telephone +44 1865 312262

Raintree is an imprint of Capstone Global Library Limited, a company incorporated in England and Wales having its registered office at 7 Pilgrim Street, London, EC4V 6LB – Registered company number: 6695582

Text © Capstone Global Library Limited 2011
First published in hardback in 2011
First published in paperback in 2012
The moral rights of the proprietor have been asserted.

Edited by Dan Nunn, Rebecca Rissman, and Sian Smith
Designed by Joanna Hinton-Malivoire
Picture research by Elizabeth Alexander
Originated by Capstone Global Library Ltd
Printed and bound in China by Leo Paper Products Ltd

ISBN 978 1 406 22051 3 (hardback)
15 14 13 12 11
10 9 8 7 6 5 4 3 2 1

ISBN 978 1 406 22338 5 (paperback)
16 15 14 13 12 11
10 9 8 7 6 5 4 3 2 1

British Library Cataloguing in Publication Data
Guillain, Charlotte.
  My first sleepover. – (Growing up)
  1. Sleepovers–Pictorial works–Juvenile literature.
  I. Title II. Series
  793.2′1-dc22

Acknowledgements
We would like to thank the following for permission to reproduce photographs: Alamy pp. 12 (© Image Source), 14, 23 glossary homesick (© Catchlight Visual Services); © Capstone Publishers Ltd pp. 5, 7, 11, 19, 23 glossary host (Karon Dubke); Corbis pp. 4, 23 glossary relative (© JLP/Jose L. Pelaez), 9 (© Tony Metaxas/Asia Images), 15 (© Christina Kennedy/fstop), 16 (© Nicole Hill/Rubberball); Getty Images pp. 6 (Digital Vision), 10 (Jupiterimages/FoodPix), 13 (Jupiterimages/Brand X Pictures); Photolibrary pp. 8 (Corbis), 17 (SW Productions/Brand X Pictures), 18 (Juice Images); Shutterstock pp. 20 (© Vasiliy Koval), 21, 23 glossary operation (© Monkey Business Images).

Front cover photograph of girls at a sleepover reproduced with permission of Alamy (© Image Source). Back cover photographs of a bathroom reproduced with permission of © Capstone Publishers (Karon Dubke), and camping reproduced with permission of Shutterstock (© Vasiliy Koval).

Every effort has been made to contact copyright holders of material reproduced in this book. Any omissions will be rectified in subsequent printings if notice is given to the publisher.

Disclaimer
All the Internet addresses (URLs) given in this book were valid at the time of going to press. However, due to the dynamic nature of the Internet, some addresses may have changed or ceased to exist since publication. While the author and publisher regret any inconvenience this may cause readers, no responsibility for any such changes can be accepted by either the author or the publisher.

Contents

Some words are shown in bold, **like this**.
You can find them in the glossary on page 23.

What is a sleepover?

A sleepover is when you stay overnight at someone else's house.

It could be at a friend's house or with **relatives**.

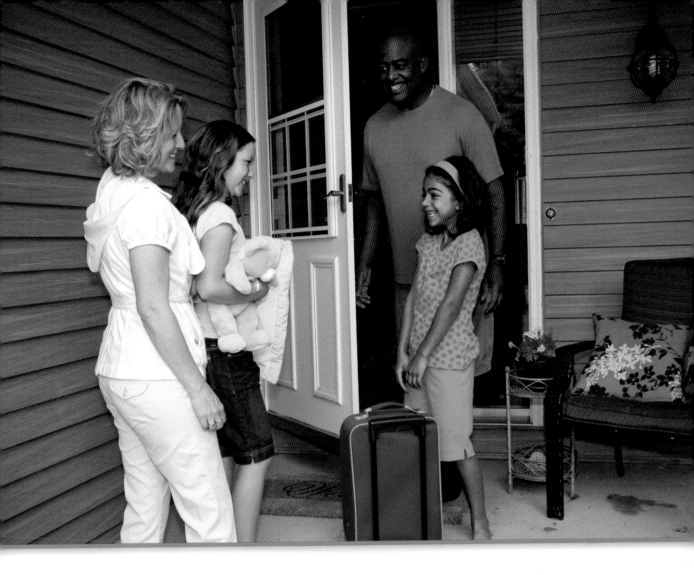

You may sleep at another house for one night, or sometimes for longer.

You may eat your evening meal and breakfast at a sleepover.

Why do people have sleepovers?

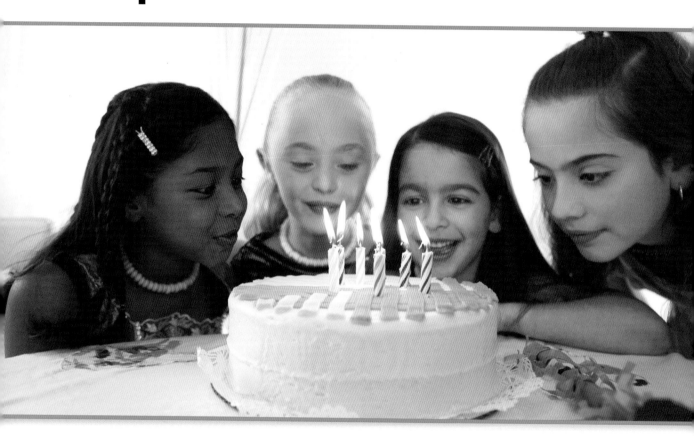

Many people have sleepovers for fun.

Some people have a sleepover with friends to celebrate their birthdays.

You may go to a sleepover with friends or family if your parents are away.

Your parents might have to go into hospital or away for work or a trip.

What do I need to take?

You need to take pyjamas, a toothbrush, and a change of clothes.

Sometimes you might also take your own sleeping bag to sleep in.

You might take something to remind you of home, such as a teddy bear or book.

You might like to take a photo of your family with you.

What do I need to know?

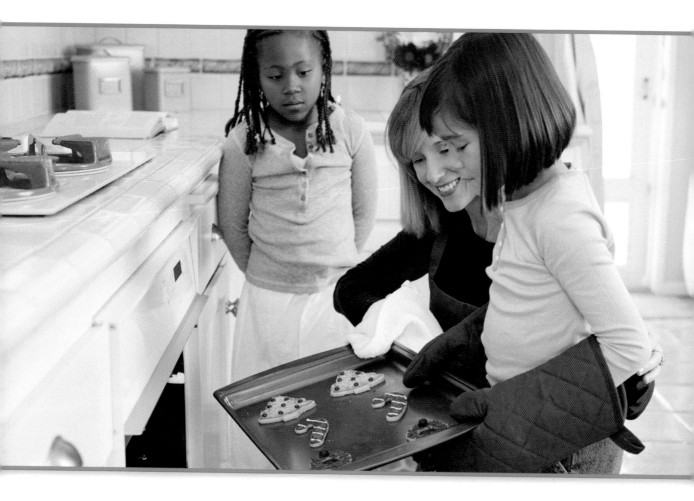

It is a good idea to know what to expect on a sleepover.

Ask your **relative** or your friend's parents what will happen during your stay.

Find out where everything is and always ask if you need anything.

Make sure you know where the toilet and bathroom are.

What might be different?

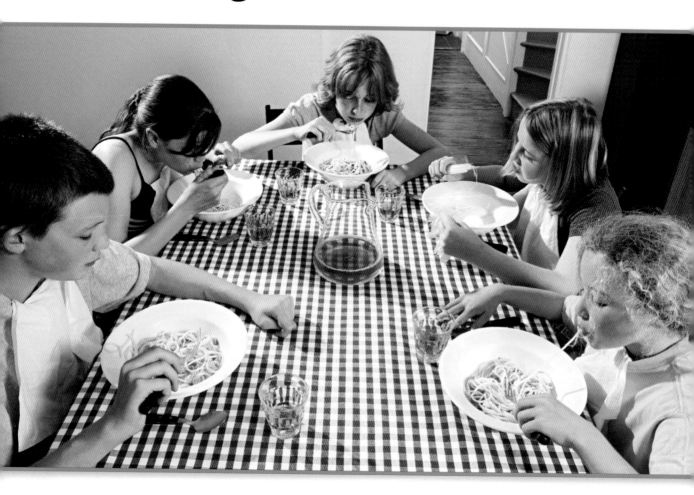

When you sleep over somewhere else, lots of things might be different.

You might try new or unusual food or eat meals at different times.

If you are staying with friends it might be exciting to stay up later than normal.

You might sleep on the floor or share a room for the first time.

What should I do if I miss home?

You might miss your family and your own bedroom at home.

Tell your **relative** or friend and his or her parents if you feel **homesick**.

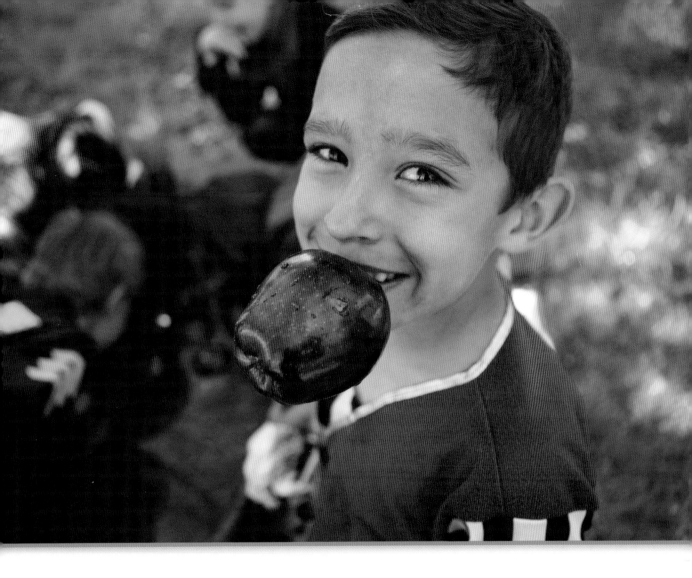

You might be able to phone your parents to make you feel better.

Try to keep busy and have fun doing something new.

What makes sleepovers fun?

Sleepovers are fun because you do things in a different way to normal.

You might eat special food together.

It is fun to see your friends in a different situation, or spend time with a **relative**.

You might play games or watch a film together.

What happens at the end?

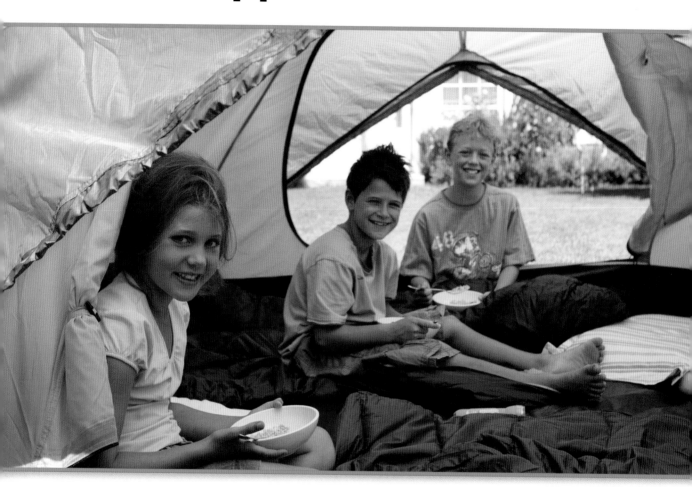

You might feel tired in the morning if you stayed up late.

You will usually have breakfast before you go home.

Make sure you remember all your things and say thank you to your **host**.

You might like to give them a gift or a card to say thank you.

When else might I stay away from home?

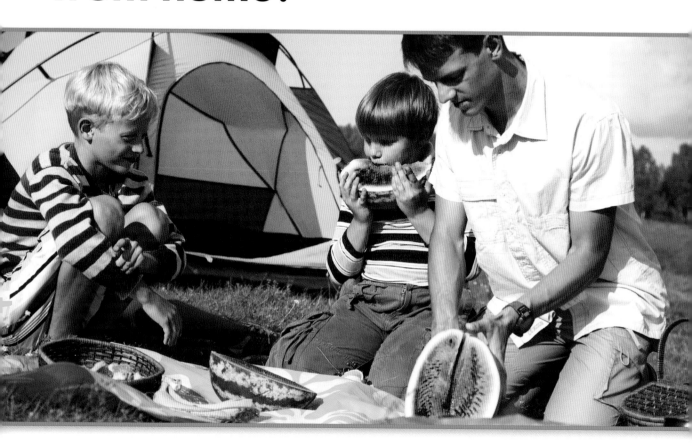

You might have to sleep away from home at other times.

You might go away on a school trip or go camping with cubs or the brownies.

If you are ill or need an **operation,** you may have to stay in hospital for a while.

If you have been on a sleepover you won't feel so nervous if this happens.

What to pack for a sleepover

- ✓ pyjamas
- ✓ a change of clothes
- ✓ toothbrush
- ✓ hairbrush
- ✓ towel
- ✓ sleeping bag
- ✓ teddy
- ✓ a gift

Picture glossary

 homesick when someone misses their home and family

 host someone you go to stay with or visit who looks after you and makes sure that you have the things you need

 operation special treatment in hospital

 relative person in your family

Find out more

Books

Harry and the Dinosaurs First Sleepover, Ian Whybrow (Puffin, 2010)

The Large Family: Sebastian's Sleepover, Jill Murphy (Walker, 2009)

Websites

You can sleepover with the dinosaurs at the Natural History Museum in London:
http://www.nhm.ac.uk/visit-us/whats-on/nights-museum-events/dino-snores

Or stay with daleks at the National Media Museum in Bradford:
http://www.nationalmediamuseum.org.uk/sleepover/home.asp

Your parents can help you find out about a sleepover in a museum near you.

Index